MISSIONS TO SUCCESS

The Beginning to Success is ALWAYS the Hardest

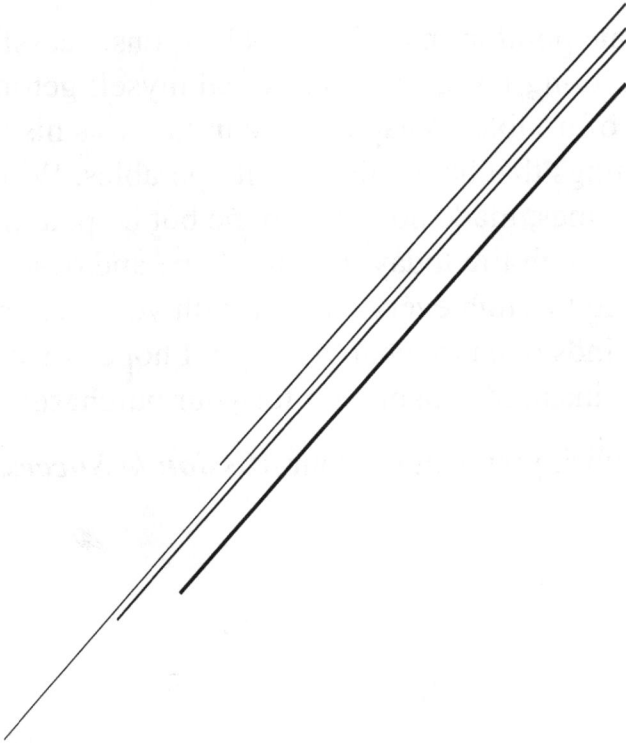

A note from the author

As you begin to read this amazing book, I want to help you understand that my grandfather John Richards aka "Grandpa Wise" is what I called him, played a massive role in my life.

At one point in my life, I was lost, unsuccessful at everything I did, and even found myself getting in a lot of trouble. What kept me in line was his many teachings that he would put into parables. Which at the times, made no sense to me but helped me to get through life today. It is my hope and desire that you go through every chapter with your hearts and minds open to what you read. I hope you are inspired. Thank you for your purchase!

I wish you well on your *Mission to Success.*

THIS BOOK IS NOT INTENDED TO BE A HISTORY TEXT. While every effort has been made to check the accuracy of dates, locations, and historical information, no claims are made as to the accuracy of such information.

For book orders, author appearance inquires and interviews, contact author: binspired52@gmail.com or www.johneunice.com

**"Keep your head up... your eyes open...
because the finish line is NEAR!"
-Brandon Oliver, Sr.**

Table of Contents

Editorial Review

Missions to Success is a breathtaking work of art. Woven through the threads of each chapter is a life lesson like no other. Brandon Oliver has the ability to take a story and make it relatable to where many of us are at any given moment. Within this book, you will find and identify with many of its paths to success. There in between the lines, you will find yourself filled with hope and ready to pursue your dreams with a new fire.

-Tasha T. Huston
Editor-In-Chief

ENTERPRISE

The "Missions To Success" Experience Reviews

"My favorite was The Pursuit of a Fish. I love how nobody could see the fish but him, because it is your dream, and nobody can see it first but YOU! I love how each story was told in a creative way. This is a book I could read over and over. The author's style of writing is very creative, and the flow of the story keeps you engaged the whole way." *-Tory Johnson*

"The book really impacted me a lot. It made me look at my failures but also look at how far I come. It helped me realize that failures are a part of life, and I will get through them. What stood out to me the most was each story had its own meaning. What's impressive about the author is that he is a "walking book." He could tell you a story like no other." *-Byron Smith*

"Overall, this book was great. I love how I could hear the author's voice and could use it in my life as a guide to success. The author has a gift of storytelling. He impressed me in how the stories were set up and you could feel as if you were going through the problems with the characters." *-Tia Orr*

"The chapter that stood out to me the most was The Test or The Party. I love the way he made it seem so real. The stories were told in a way that once you started to read it was hard to put it down because for me I wanted to know what was going to happen. The author... what could I say?! He is really creative, unique in his own way. I love how he focused on 1 problem and building a story around it. This book I would say is a must-read!!" *-Jairon Durham*

It's Time to Wake-Up

(Grandpa speaking to himself)

"Where is this grandson of mine?! I told him if we don't get a moving we're going to be late to the game. Brandon what are you doing still in bed?!

"Not now Grandpa, I am dreaming that the Oliver Hawks are leading in the 4th quarter. If you don't wake up you will never get to see if it could really happen!

"Ugh! Grandpa, you're ruining a good dream! Why waste your time on dreaming when you could spend time making it happen?" Said Grandpa.

"Move over let me tell you what happens to a person who enjoy sleeping all day.

There was once a man who had a wife and three children. He had two boys and a daughter. He loved his family so much, but he also loved to sleep. He could sleep for days. Sleeping is something that he did very well. I find it hard to sleep a lot when having a family, but this father had no problem.

The father comes in one day to his family sitting and eating dinner, he greets them and then says to them. "I'm going to sleep before work. If I sleep too long, you guys come and wake me up."

The next day arrives and the wife is cooking breakfast with the kids sitting in the kitchen getting prepared for school. She notices that Daddy is still sleeping. She turns to her children and said, "Your father is still sleep. One of you go to wake him up or he will be late to work."

The oldest son goes into the room where he finds his father sleeping and tries to wake him. "Daddy, Daddy it is time to wake up or you will be late to work."

-Father: Son leave me alone; I'm dreaming right now let me get back to my dream.

-The son goes back into the kitchen and said to his mother, "Mama, I tried to wake Daddy up, but he wouldn't get up."

The 2nd oldest son jumps out of his seat.

-2nd Son: I will go wake him up.

He walks into the room where he finds his Daddy sleeping. Starts to shake him.

-2nd son: Daddy, Daddy it's time to wake up.

The Father replied, **"did I not tell your brother that I was sleeping?! Now I am dreaming son let me get back to my dream.**

He then walks back into the kitchen to where his mother and siblings are, "Mama I also tried to wake Daddy up and he said he was dreaming."

The daughter gets out of her seat.

-Daughter: Leave it up to me, Daddy's favorite to wake him up.

-She walks in to see her Daddy sleeping and in her sweet calm little voice. "Daddy it's time to get up or you will be late for work."

-Father: Baby girl I love you, but right now Daddy is dreaming; let me get back to this dream.

-She walks back to the kitchen where she also tells them, "Daddy is focus on his dream and doesn't want to get up."

Days and days have gone by and the father is still sleeping. The kids tried everything to wake him up. They pushed him out of the bed. They poured water on him while he slept but nothing could wake him up from this dream. Until they all just stopped waking him up because they realized ***Daddy's dreaming.***

Well, finally the father wakes up from his dream to realize that he is late for work. He jumps up and runs to the kitchen. He finds his wife and kids at the table getting ready for school.

-Father: Why didn't anybody wake me up like I asked you guys to?

-They all sat and looked, as he looked at them. The phone rings and it is his boss from work. The father picks up.

-Father: Hello.

-Boss: Hey John, we were just wondering about you. You haven't been to work in a few days.

-Father: I can explain that. I will be right there.

-Boss: Well, no need you have not been to work in some time now. We were just calling to let you know we decided to let you go.

-Father: Well, that is not necessary, I just - overslept.

-Boss: I am sorry, but that is it.

The father hangs up and now he is mad.

He walks back to the kitchen where his family is all gathered.

-Father: Kids I just lost my job because you did not wake me up, how am I supposed to take care of bills? How am I supposed to take care of this house?

The father went on and on about losing his job, as the kids and wife looked on. His wife finally stops him.

*"Are you done? Let me tell you something every day the kids tried to wake you up, but you thought that sleep was more important. You woke up when you realized that we were no longer waking you up. The truth is when you want something in life nobody must wake you up. The dream that you went to sleep and saw was so good you did not want to wake up. So, **YOU** lost your job. Is it our job to wake you up? If I can be honest with you, it is when you want something in life you wake up every day on your own. The dream is showing you what you could have. It is the choices you make that will determine your outcome. It is our duty when we are given a gift, a dream, a passion we*

must wake up every day and pursue the very thing we saw, If not then we are still sleeping.

Okay Grandpa, **you win.** That's my cue, I am up," said Brandon.

"Oh no. You should stay sleep. What happen to your dream is so much better?"

"I learned that I rather make it my reality than to only dream about it. I don't want to spend the rest of my life dreaming of something I could achieve."

A dream is something you go to sleep to see, but reality is something you must wake up to. Make your dream a reality and that requires you to wake up.

It is Time to Wake Up.

Marriage vs. Divorce

I think it is okay to say we have all been to a wedding at least once. So what exactly is a marriage? It is two people who becomes a union or partners. I would say: two people, who make a commitment for richer or poor, sickness and in health to stay together at all cost. What about a divorce? That's simply, to me, means to split or to just give up. Here, I will explain what I mean by marriage and divorce.

"That's it! I had it! I am not playing football anymore," said Brandon.

"What seems to be the problem?" Grandpa Wise asked.

"No matter how hard I train, I never get picked to play with the other guys."

"You can't just give up, keep trying."

"No I had it! I quit!"

"Why would you quit something you love?"

"Grandpa, things are not going my way!"

"Let me tell you something; things will never go as planned, but you don't just give up. *You must keep going.* I think I should tell you about this couple I knew…

(They sat down.)

There was a couple by the names of John and Eunice. They had been married for many years. John worked on the railroad. Every day he worked from sun up until sundown. He made sure all the bills were paid, and his wife was happy. Eunice did most of her work around the house. She enjoyed cooking and making sure the house was clean when John came home from working all day. For this was the agreement that they both made. John and Eunice loved one another and understood their roles very well. They always did what was best for each other and for their marriage.

One day Eunice was on the way home then BOOM! She was in a bad accident.

This led her to being in a wheelchair. It limited her from doing all the things she was able to do in the beginning. John loved Eunice so much that he stopped working as much to take care of her. He now found himself working, cooking, cleaning, and now making sure the house was comfortable for Eunice while she stayed home.

John is working early in the morning, coming home, cooking, cleaning, and making sure Eunice is taken care of. Eunice is seeing how everyday John's working, taking care of her, it started to make her think that John was overworking himself. He comes home one day and Eunice is sitting in the kitchen. *"John, I know that you're working hard and I don't want to be a burden on you. So maybe you should just divorce me."*

John replied "Baby it's no problem. I signed up for this."

"No, John you don't understand. You had to reduce your hours from the work you love. You are cooking, cleaning, everything that I'm supposed to be doing for you, is now all on you."

John replied "Baby, it's no problem."

John would do his same routine every day. He would work, cook, and clean. Everything he needed to do for the wife that he loved. *Eunice felt different.* She felt like she meant him no good at all.

"Baby, you're working too hard! You just need to divorce me! Look at me! I can't help you like I want to.

(Eunice began to cry.)

All the time, John would tell Eunice "It's okay baby I'm built for this."

She went on and on about him leaving her and him finding someone that could help him. John had finally had enough.

"How come ***every*** time I come home you tell me I need to divorce you?"

"Well, John look at me. I can't cook for you. I can't clean. I can't do nothing for you!"

"Eunice, I'm not leaving you! Because when I married you I made a commitment to you. When you love something, you don't give up on it so easily. Yes some things are hard on me, but I made **a commitment** to you and to myself. It's easy for me to divorce you and give up, but that's not my motto. I'm going to stick it out because I love you too much to just leave. Eunice when I married you, I didn't marry you because you could cook, clean, or take care of the house. *I married you because of the man you made me.* You made me better. When times were hard you didn't give up on me so I'm not giving up on you. You see marriage is a commitment, while divorce means to give up. I am not going anywhere because I am committed to what it is that I love…

You see Brandon, things didn't go John's way. But he never gave up on Eunice. He stayed committed to what he loved.

Eunice asked him many times to divorce her and move on with his life. For John, marriage was a commitment, and that is what it will take when things don't go as plan. John could've gave Eunice what she wanted, but he didn't see himself giving up on her, and that is how you should see things you want out of life. *If you love it, don't give up, because it will soon get better.*"

Are you married to the process, or are you about to divorce it?

Hold up!

You're thinking too quickly. At this time, I want you to stop and first ask yourself, "Why did I start in the first place?" If you're thinking like me, nothing will go as planned, and you have to ask yourself, "What drives me to keep going? Why does quitting even cross my mind?"

If I can leave you with anything it's my famous slogan.

"Whatever you do, just see it through."

It means whatever you start, I dare you to finish it. If you are committing to something stay committed. It is so much easier to divorce meaning to give up when things do not go as planned.

I encourage you to keep moving, do not quit, push through, and *if you love it... you will stay committed.*

The Pursuit of a Fish

Have you ever told someone your dream and they told you "they didn't see it happening."

I bet it crushed your heart that they didn't see what you saw. The point is that everyone **can't see** what is only meant for you. The real question is, *will you still pursue what you saw?*

"We've been on this lake for hours Grandpa, and I still haven't seen any fish. I am starting to believe there are no fish."

"Just hold tight, it takes a while."

"But Grandpa you said you saw a bunch of fish and I haven't seen not one."

"Well, maybe it is not meant for you to see."

"What do you mean *it is not meant* for me to see?"

"Brandon, there will be some things in life you will not understand, but only the one who saw it for themselves. I think this is a great time to tell you about a lake long ago called *Lake Never.*

Once upon a time in a small little ole county town there was this lake. The lake was called "Lake

*Never." It gained its name because this lake, since the beginning of time, was known for not having any fish; not even one. Well, one day this young man was walking by the lake. He looks at the lake, and he saw a fish jump out the water and back in. He was so amazed and excited. He begins to run back into town to tell everyone he had seen a fish in Lake Never. Everyone laughed because they all knew "Lake Never **never** produced any fish." He looked around wondering why everyone was laughing at him. He went home that day, and he decided that he was going to show everyone that <u>he</u> knew he saw a fish. The next day he goes to the bank he takes some money out. He was going to buy a boat and some fishing products to prove to everyone that it's a fish in the lake. In order to get a boat and some fishing products he had to go far away. No one in this small town has ever been fishing in Lake Never. They had no fishing nor boat shops in town.*

Finally, after gathering everything he needed, he gets the boat and fishing products and heads back into town. While he was driving back into town, the town people would look at him crazy because nobody owned a boat in this town. *This was crazy to even see a boat drive into town like this, but that didn't stop him.* The following day he gets the boat ready to put out on the lake. He sails out on the lake, throwing his fishing line out waiting for this fish to bite so he could catch it and bring it back to show to the town's people. Just then, the line starts to get tight. The fish is on the line, but the fish was so strong it took the whole fishing pole. He realized that this wasn't just a small fish, this was a **big fish**.

He goes back to the fishing store and ask the worker.
"Do you have anything a little stronger to catch big fish?"
"Well, of course I do."
"How about this one right here?" Matthew replied
"I will take it."

While coming back into town, he stops at the store and people would make fun of him because he was trying to catch a fish that was never in the lake. A little girl saw him and said,

"Look it's the guy who said he saw a fish in lake!"

The whole store turns and looks and start to make fun of him for trying to catch something that's not there.

Matthew ended up running into a friend and he asked him, "How are you coming with catching the fish you saw?"

Matthew said, "This is no little fish. This is a very big fish."

"Ha-ha! Sure it is," his friend laughed.
"You know what?! I'm going back out to the lake soon. Come with me, and I will show you what I saw."

The friend agrees to go, as they are now putting stuff in the boat, preparing to sail out to the middle of the lake. Matthew's at the front while his friend is in the back of the boat.

"Friend, so where's this fish?"
"Matthew, just be patient you will see it soon."

It takes so long that the sun is starting to go down, and the friend is starting to fall asleep. It's now nighttime, and the friend is in the back of the boat asleep.

Just then... the fish jumps up out of the water.

Matthew's eyes are about to pop out of his head seeing how big this fish really is. He runs to the back of the boat to wake up his friend.

"Wake up! Wake up! The fish... the fish!"
Just as the friend wakes up and runs to the front of the boat, the fish jumps back into the water, and

the water becomes still as if nothing happened. The friend becomes upset.

"I knew it wasn't a fish in this water! You are crazy just like everyone said. This lake is called "Lake Never" for a reason. Take me back. I knew it. I shouldn't have come out with you! *It was a crazy idea.*"

Matthew takes his friend back to town, where the friend wishes him well on catching a fish that's not there.

"Good luck on catching your imaginary fish."

Matthew has a look of disappointment on his face. He then gets an idea. He returned to the fish shop.

"I need the strongest fishing pole you have."
"Are you sure that you can afford it?" Cashier replies.
"Yes!"
"Well, it's not a regular pole. It's a cane pole where it's your strength against the fish."
"I will take it."
"Dude, are you sure you want to spend this much on a fishing pole?"
"I'm willing to risk it all to catch this fish."
"Alright," he hands Matthew the fishing pole, "Here you go, good luck."

Matthew now sets out on a journey that no matter what, *he's not coming back empty-handed*.

He packs enough food for days because he made up his mind that he wasn't coming back until he catches this fish that *he knew* he saw.

He's now in the lake with his cane pole in position. It's starting to get late, and the sun is going down. The days are flying by fast. Day after day, month after month, year after year, and Brandon's still out trying to catch the fish he saw.

Just as dawn breaks, a pull on the line, and it's the fish that Brandon knew that he saw so long ago. Brandon is pulling with all his might, but the fish is not making it easy. They are both pulling away from one another. The town's people are riding by. They see him pulling as if he has something. Everyone knows it's the crazy man that claims he saw a fish.

Days go by, and Matthew is still pulling; he's not giving up because he knew he wanted to show everyone what he saw was true. He's pulling and pulling, until all of a sudden the fish stops pulling.

Matthew pulls the fish on the boat and he realizes that this fish is bigger then what it looks. It's so heavy that the boat is starting to sink because of the weight of the fish. He tries to hurry back to town to show everyone the fish that he saw. The fish end up being one of the largest catches ***in history***.

The news people interviewed him.

"I was walking and saw the fish jump out of the water. Nobody believed me when I said I saw a fish in the lake. I knew I had to show them what I saw."

"Wow! That's amazing story Grandpa. The fact Matthew saw the fish and nobody else could. What makes it even better is that he went after it."

"That's right!" Grandpa Wise replied. "Remember this… there will be times in life you will dream, and these could be some really big dream; and everyone might not be able to understand them. BUT you can't let that stop you from pursuing what you saw. See it, believe it, and go after it."

With the lake now having its first fish ever, the lake was renamed, ***Lake Hope***. Everyone had hope they could catch a fish as big as this one.

Matthew went on to open a boat and fishing shop. Everyone in town bought all their items from him, hoping to catch a fish as big as his.

The pursuit of a fish is to go for your dreams even when you're the only one who sees it.

No one will see your dream as clear as you will.

Focus on the Road

There comes a time when every parent or someone you look up to will teach you how to drive. And this day, it was Grandpa Wise's turn to teach Brandon.

"Boy, if you don't sit your seat upright and put your seat belt on! You don't just get in the car and get comfortable, like you been driving for years."

"Ugh!!! Come on Grandpa! That's the style now."

"Well you style in your own car! This here is mine. Fix your mirrors. Boy, I tell you these kids today. Hold up! What do you think you're doing?"

"Grandpa, I got this. I been practicing."

"Practicing where?"

"This game called *Grand Theft Auto;* it's a driving game."

"Driving is not a game. It can cost you your life if you're not focused. Cut the car off, let me tell you about a time a buddy of mine didn't take driving so serious…

Alright son, this is the day I'm going to teach you how to drive.", The father replied. Now, son I want you to understand it's not just about getting in the car and going, but there are some rules that you have to follow when it comes to driving. First, always put your seat belt on. Second, you want to check both side mirrors to the left and the right of you. You want to make sure that you're able to see out of them. Third, on the right is the gas pedal, it allows you to move. On the left are the brakes, they allow you to stop or slow down. Fourth, in front of you is the wheel, this will allow you to drive and what steers the car. The last and final thing I will tell you, Son is to focus on the road ahead of you. I repeat!! Keep your eyes on the road.

-Son: Dad I got this.

-Father: Son listen to me, KEEP YOUR EYES ON THE ROAD!!

Months had gone by. The Son, with the help of his father, had been riding around and practicing. He was finally ready to go out on his own.

-Son: Hey Dad! I am getting ready to head out and meet some of my friends.

-Father: Okay Son, just remember what I said, seat belt.

-Son: Yea Dad, I got you. I promise you.

-Father: Son, whatever you do, just make sure you focus on the road.

He is now driving, and while he is driving, his phone begins to ring on the seat next to him. While he is driving, he starts to reach for it taking his eyes off the road. He makes a mistake and knocks the phone on the floor. Now, he is reaching for the phone, looking at the road, and looking down at the floor. He's trying to pay attention to the road. He's reaching down, and he finally gets the phone. He looks up in time to see he's about to run right into a truck. He quickly swerves off the road into a ditch. The car comes to a complete stop. He makes his way out of the car with his phone in his hand and unharmed with just a little soreness. The car was beat up, and he was happy to make it out alive. He makes a phone call to his Father.

-Son: Hey Dad. I was in a wreck. I need you to get here quick.

The father arrives to the scene to a whole bunch of police and ambulances. He runs up to his son.

-Father: Son, are you okay? What happened?

-Son: Dad, I took…

The father cuts him off before he could even get his sentence out.

-Father: Son, did a tire blow, or did someone almost hit you?

-Son: No.

-Father: Well, what happened?

-Son: (takes a deep breath) My phone started to ring, and when I went to reach for it. It fell to the floor. The phone was still ringing, and I was still looking at the road. At the same time, I was trying to reach for the phone. I looked up, and I almost hit a truck in the back. It caused me to swerve off the road and into the ditch.

-Father: Son, thank God you came out alive, but I thought I told you whatever you do to focus on the road.

-Son: I know Dad. I know you're disappointed in me.

-Father: Son, I am not disappointed in you; I am just happy you made it out alive.

Months later, the father shows up with a new car for his son.

-Son: Whose car is this Dad?

-Father: Son, it's yours.

-Son: But Dad, what if I wreck this car like the last time?

-Father: Son, let me tell you something. In life, we will always make mistakes, and that means even losing focus at times. You cannot let that deter you from getting back out there again. Son, all you did was lose your focus. *You must remember,* no matter what happens, don't you ever take your eyes off the road. I do not care who calls you. I would rather you have a missed call then for me to have a son who I would miss. Son, yes you lost your focus and ended up in a ditch, but it did not kill you. It made you aware of where your focus was. So, you get in this car and you make sure you keep your eyes on the road. No matter what happens, don't you lose focus of what's in front of you being too busy looking at what's around you at something that is not going to help you get to your destination.

You see Brandon my friend was lucky enough to make it out alive. What cause him to wreck was when he took his focus off the road, worried about the things that didn't matter. So, son I know sometimes you will lose focus but I want you to always remember *let nothing distract you from getting to your destination."*

It is clear that a phone does have a GPS on it, but it wasn't the GPS he was going after. The phone fell to the ground and the call was more important than watching the road.

If I can be honest, we all have been distracted by something that has taken our eyes off our destination. I encourage you to keep your eyes on whatever your road is. *Do not be afraid to get back on the road again once you have gained your focus.*

The Test or the Party

Choices - when facing two or more possibilities; having to only pick one.

(Brandon walks over to Grandpa.)

"Grandpa, I am having a hard time choosing between my favorite red shirt and this black one, which I really want to wear."

"Sounds like you're going to have to make a choice."

"What's a choice? Brandon asked."

"A choice is having to pick between two things but could only pick one. Don't worry, let me explain? I will tell you about a time I had to make one of the biggest decisions of my life.

There were two boys by the name of Jacob and Brian. They were friends since they were kids. They did everything together. They were so close if you saw one you saw the other. Along the way, the two of them stayed very close friends. Brian went off to college while Jacob stayed back and decided school was not for him. Being miles away did not affect the bond they had with one another. On this day, Jacob made a phone call to Brian.

-Jacob: "Yo Brian! Big news! There's a big party and I know you're always down to party."

-Brian: "You know I'm always down for a party and you know we don't party without one another, when is it? Brian replied.

-Jacob: "It's the 12th, in a few days" Jacob replied.

 -Brian: "The 12th! Aww man I don't know. I have a test coming up that's on the 13th early in the morning."

-Jacob: "Oh man, now you know we don't party without one another. Forget about the test; you can always do it another time."

-Brian: "Yea, but this test is really important to me, and this will allow me to get into my career program."

-Jacob: "Okay, I get it, but look, you have a few days just think on it, and I will call you back."

At this time, Brian's mother walks in to see him at the table and noticed he is acting a little strangely as if he was thinking about something. One thing about a mother, you cannot get nothing pass them.

-Mother: "Why the long face?" she replied.

-Brian: "Ugh! Well, I have a test on the 13th, and Jacob wants me to attend this party on the 12th with him."

-Mother: "Oh, Jacob, you guys have been friends for years. I tell you if you see him, you saw you. Y'all always doing things together.

-Brian: "Yes, I know, but I don't know what to do."

-Mother: "Well son, you know I am not the one to say what you should do, but just make the best decision for yourself."

A call comes in on Brian's phone, and it's Jacob.

-Jacob: "Hey B! My man, what's the deal?"

-Brian: "Well Jacob, I thought about it, and I am going to have to pass on this one. The test is more important right now."

-Jacob: "That's how you do me?! You know we do everything together. Over a dumb test?! You know how important this party is and you don't want to go?! *What kind of friend are you?*" Jacob begins to argue and starts to yell.

-Brian: "You know what? I never want to be your friend again!" he hangs up the phone, never to hear from Jacob again.

Months had gone by, and Brian's test results have finally come in. He opens them up, and to his surprise, all the hard work paid off!

He passed his test! He runs to his mother to tell her the good news.

-Brian: "Mother... Mother, I passed my test! I passed my test! I am finally in my program of study."

Even though he's excited about his test, he becomes sad because he used to share all his good news with his best friend, Jacob. He no longer wanted to be friends with him anymore all because he made a decision not to attend the party and study instead.

He started to cry.

On one hand, he passed his test, but on the other hand, he no longer had his friend of many years. His mother looked at him.

-Mother: "Baby, dry your eyes because you passed your test. Yes, you might be a little hurt that you lost your friend of many years, but you made the best decision that was going to benefit you. Had he been a real friend, he would've encouraged you to focus on your test and not on a party. Son, sometimes you must be willing to make sacrifices. They are going to cost you something. You must be willing to let some things, and even some people go to get to the place that you're destined to be. Yes, you lost your friend, but you passed your test because you knew what was best for you. Son I became a mother at a young age. I lost a lot of friends because *I made the choice* to take care of you. I skipped out on parties, and had to get a full-time job. I laid down my life so that I could give you a better life. I am proud of myself. I made the sacrifice that was going to better myself and your life. So, son, cry if you must but wipe those tears away. There will be many more times in your life you will have to make a choice. The biggest part of being a mother is the *sacrifice* we give up for our children to have a better life.

So Brandon, to answer your question, you should pick your favorite one. You could never go wrong with the one you love the most. I want you to remember this… in life, we will always have to make sacrifices, and these sacrifices will either help or hurt us, *but* you have to always do what is best for you.

This story is dedicated to my loving mother, Dolphanie Richards. Mother, I thank you for your many sacrifices. You were willing to lose for your children to gain. You laid down your life so that you could give your children (Jairon, Tia, Tory, Renee, Jada, and myself) a better life, and not one time did we hear you complain. You made all the right choices for us, and for that, I want to say, **I love you** *for putting our needs in front of your wants.*

12 Rounds of Life

There will be times in your *life* when you feel defeated. It becomes hard picking yourself up after being knocked down so many times. Can I tell you a secret, you might be down, but <u>*you are not*</u> out.

(Brandon looks confused.)

"Grandpa, why won't this guy just stay down? He has been knocked down almost every round of the fight."

"True, but it is never over until he stops getting up," Grandpa Wise replied.

"It is no way he could win."

"I wouldn't speak so fast Brandon anything could happen."

"Oh yea?! Who do you know that has ever come back from a fight like this?"

"I actually do know someone who has. Let me think, it was in 1970 or was in the 80s? OH! I got it.

I had a friend whose son was an amateur boxer. He had been boxing for a while but never had a real boxing match. One day, he and a group of his friends went into a gym. The son was punching the punching bag and making loud noise. Some would even say he was like a young Muhammad Ali yelling "I'm the greatest!!" "Who want to fight me?" Well, we all know you always get what you ask for.

A few other guys listening to his loud yelling walked over to see what all the fuss was about.

"Aye man!! What is all this yelling about?" Shouted one of the guys from the group.

-Son: I am just so excited about being back in the gym, and I am looking for someone to fight.

"This man does not know who I am." The guy looks around to his friends, and said:

-Son: I'm just looking for a fight. I will fight anybody. You pick them.

Everyone started to laugh at him.

"This man *really* does not know who I am." Stated the guy in the group.

"Anybody know that if you are looking for a fight, you must first go through me. People like you I don't have to prepare for, but I will give you 2 months to train. We will meet back here to fight.

-Son: Alright, my 1st fight, can I get your name?

"This man *really* does not know who I am?! My name is LIFE!!!"

He is so excited for his first fight he runs over to his friends to tell them the news.

-Son: Guess what? I have my first fight in 2 months.

-Friends: A fight! A fight with who?

-Son: He said his name was Life.

His friends looked shocked because they knew he did not know what he was getting himself into.

-Friend: You said you are about to fight Life?

-Son: Yea, I'm about to fight Life in 2 months.

-Friend: Man, you might want to tell him you were just playing. Life is no joke. Life will knock you out. From what I heard, a lot of people don't even make it out the ring.

-Son: Man, I got this. Just be here in 2 months.

-Friend: Well, I guess we need to get our black suits ready as well.

The son runs off to the barbershop. He is from a very small town where everyone knows everyone. While he is getting a haircut, his barber engaged in a conversation with him.

-Barber: How everything been?

-Son: It's great.

-Barber: How you doing with boxing?

-Son: Man, you will never believe it! I have my first match in 2 months to a guy name Life.

The barber stops cutting his hair, and the whole barbershop gets quiet.

-Barber: Son you about to fight who?

-Son: Life.

-Barber: Son, you might want to tell him you were just playing when you challenged him. Life is no joke, and from what I heard if Life Jr. is anything like his Daddy, Life Sr... *He will knock you out.*

After his haircut, he arrives at home still excited. He runs to his mother and tells her the good news.

-Son: Mother, you will not believe it. I have my first fight in two months.

-Mother: That's good baby, who are you fighting?

-Son: He said his name was Life?

The mother instantly starts crying. She knew her baby did not know what he was getting himself into.

-Mother: Son, go in there and tell your father what you about to do.

He walks in to find his father with his glasses on and reading the newspaper.

-Son: Father, you would be so proud of me. I have my first boxing match.

-Father: Son, that's great with who?

-Son: His name is Life.

The father puts the newspaper down and removes his glasses.

-Father: Son, do you know what you are getting yourself into? Life is no joke. He will knock you out. You are my son. Let me prepare you for the fight.

The father makes a phone call to his longtime friend by the name of Believe.

-Father: Hey, Believe what is going on? I know I have not talked to you in a long time, but my son is about to have his first fight, and he needs a trainer.

-Believe: For you I will do anything. Let me ask you, who is he about to fight?

-Father: He is about to fight Life.

-Believe: What?! He stops and takes a deep breath. You know what… for you I will do it.

Believe lived far away. To get to his house, you would have to take a train, a plane, and a boat just to get there. Once he arrived, he knocks on the door.

"Knock Knock." Believe opens the door and he walks in.

-Son: I'm so excited that you're going to train me.

Believe stops him from talking.

-Believe: First off, if I'm going to train you, I need you to do everything I tell you and don't say nothing to me. Now, in the back, it's a treadmill. *Run* until I tell you to stop.

The son is running on the treadmill for hours before Believe rushes in, turns the machine off, and sends him home.

This trip was no short trip. In order for him to get back home, he had to take the same boat, plane, and train to get there.

Every day the son did this for weeks and weeks. He would run on the treadmill for hours and sometimes days, until he realized he hadn't thrown a punch yet. All he was doing was running. He thought to himself *how am supposed to win if I haven't thrown a punch.*

Boxing is not about running, but it's about the punches that you land. He thought to himself. I know Believe don't want me to ask him anything, but I must ask.

The son gets to Believe house.

-Son: Hey, I know I'm not supposed to ask you anything, but how am I going to win if I haven't thrown a punch?

Believe turns around.

-Believe: Son, when I first started training you, I told you not to ask me anything. Now in the back, it's a treadmill, run until I tell you to stop.

Again, he is on this treadmill for a few hours until Believe rushes in, turns the machine off, and sends him home.

The day has finally come before the fight and the son went over to Believe's house for the last time. He gets on the treadmill and in rushes Believe. He turns the machine off and sent him home.

-Believe: Son, go home. You have a big fight tomorrow, and you're going to need your rest. As he's walking out the door he turns to Believe.

-Son: Believe, I know I didn't invite you to come to my match tomorrow, but you're welcome to come.

Believe looks at him.

-Believe: I will think about it.

The day of the fight and the entire town is in attendance. The barbershop, grocery stores, and everything else is closed. Everybody is at the fight for one thing they knew was going to happen; Life was going to knock the son out. They wanted to be there to support the father when his son got knocked out.

The bell goes off for the start of the first round, and Life comes out swinging.

The first few punches connected and knocks the son down.

Second and third round, he gets knocked down.

Round after round, he was knocked down all the way until the ninth round.

What is amazing about this fight is that each time he gets knocked down, he gets back up every single time. He is throwing punches here and there. Life is bigger, stronger, and his boxing IQ is better.

Before the tenth round, the son notices that Believe, his trainer, has walked in. That is not the only thing he's noticing. Life is tired. He's not used to going so many rounds.

If you knew Life, he would knock you out between the second to fifth round. He manages to make it to the ninth. Could he have a chance?

It is the start of the tenth round, and Life's punches are coming. They are not as fast as they were in the first couple of rounds. He is getting a few punches in. Life is still swinging and if he connects the son is going down.

Just then, Life lands a punch and down he goes again. How in the world can he win after being knocked down so many times?

The eleventh round was no different, but he got back up prepared for the last round. The twelfth round and Believe, his trainer, must have been mad because he jumps into the ring, moved his trainers out the way, and starting yelling.

-Believe: Son! You come too far! Finish what you started and remember what I taught you.

The son is thinking to himself, I did not do anything but run, but he nodded as if he knew what it was.

The last round of the fight and the son notices again that Life is tired. His punches are coming slower than the other rounds.

The son started to find his feet a little. He is punching and moving, but Life lands a punch and he goes down again.

Twelve rounds of being knocked down.

With only a minute left, the son gets back up. This time he gets up with a different attitude. He's landing punches, throwing everything he had at Life, and then something happened.

He hit Life with a right and down goes Life!

Life tried to get back up, but he couldn't find his feet, and the referee waves the fight off. The son had knocked Life out! The crowd was going crazy because no one had ever knocked Life out!

The son is so worn out, but the commentators rushed to interview him.

-Commentator: Son, you did something no one has ever done before. You knocked Life out. How did you do it?

-Son: Every day I went to my Trainer's house, who name was Believe, and in order to get there I had to take a train, a plane and a boat. When I arrived there, he would make me run on this treadmill for hours, and sometimes days. He would make me run until he told me to stop. So, every time I got knocked down, I didn't hear my trainer tell me to stop. Every time I took a blow, I didn't hear my trainer tell me to stop. I knew that Life was known to knock people out between the second to fifth rounds, so I knew if I could just make it to the sixth round, I knew I had a chance to win.

I knew Life's opponents when they got knocked down, they did not get up. I knew every time I got up; he became frustrated that I kept getting up. I knew if I just believed and outlasted Life, I could win. I did just that.

You see, Brandon that's why you should never count someone out. Remember this, it is not how many times you get knocked down, but *how many times can you get back up.* Some stay down, and some choose to get back up, but the whole picture is if you could just outlast whatever you face, you could win."

Imagine yourself on the treadmill and having to run for hours and sometimes days. Can you imagine how tired you would be? No matter how many times he got knocked off the treadmill, he got back up. Remember every time Believe came to cut the machine off, he was still running.

I want you to remember this **"Life is like a treadmill, don't you get off until your creator and trainer tells you to stop."** KEEP RUNNING!!

Keynotes:

1. Believe You Can Do It.
2. Get up when you've been knocked down.
3. Never stop believing.

Who Runs Your Neighborhood?

There was a time in my life when my Grandpa *would always* ask me, "What are you thinking about?" or "What's going on in your mind?"

I was 13 years old when he asked, and I couldn't even tell you because at this time, I was lost. One day, Grandpa asked me a question that caught me off guard.

"Who runs your neighborhood?" He asked.

He would go on to say, *"Your mind is like your neighborhood.* You control where you stay and the people you stay around. You could also be of help or bring harm to your neighborhood. You could believe life is great or live in fear of the unknown, but you must know who runs your neighborhood, which is <u>your mind</u>."

Grandpa Wise was much of a storyteller, so when he felt like you didn't understand, you best believe he followed up in a way you would understand.

"Sit down, let me tell you a story.

It was a military family that was known for moving from state to state. After finally getting settled, in this new little town which was a very good neighborhood, they were met with a not-so-nice issue.

These "new to the neighborhood brothers" were the Success brothers. One named Believe, while the other name was Conquer. They did not have a lot of friends, which helped the two brothers to become very close. The brothers were very skilled at basketball.

One day a group of neighborhood kids, about 4 of them, were walking by and spotted them playing a pickup game of basketball.

-Kid: "Hey, you guys can't be out here playing basketball in this neighborhood!" one kid shouted.

The boys stop playing to introduce themselves to the kids.

Believe: "Hi, we're the Success brothers." My name is Believe, and this is my brother Conquer.

-Kid: "Yes, we know who you are. We came over to let you guys know that nobody is allowed to play basketball without running it by **Fear and Failure.** Those guys run this neighborhood, and they're known for beating everyone in basketball. They beat me so bad I never want to play again."

-Kid 2: "They beat me so bad I never want to see another ball again."

-Believe & Conquer: Well, we're new in town, and we don't know them. If you guys don't mind, we're going to get back to our game."

The neighborhood kids were amazed at how well The Success brothers could play. Every time they would score or do something amazing, the kids would shout so loud.

Next door to the court lived Fear and Failure, the two brothers who ran the neighborhood. After hearing all the noise outside, they jumped up to see what all the fuss was about.

Out the door they ran to the sound of a ball bouncing and cheering. Just as Fear and Failure were coming up to the crowd of people, one of the neighborhood kids spotted them, and began to alert the other kids around him.

As they came close, the neighborhood kids instantly started to tell them how they tried to tell the brothers about the way this neighborhood was.

Fear and Failure looked at the Success brothers.

-Fear & Failure: "Didn't they tell you that we run this neighborhood? To even bounce a ball, you have to play us first. You know what?! Since you two want to do what you want, here is the deal. We play tomorrow, and when we win, we take your ball, and you can *never play basketball again.*"

The Success brothers looked at each other.

-Believe & Conquer: "Let's do this."

On game day, some of the neighborhood kids were out talking about the game that would take place later.

-Kid 1: "Do you think that The Success brothers have a chance to win?"

-Kid 2: "Not at all! Listen, we all know the outcome. Fear and Failure are going to do what they did to all of us out here.

-Kid 1: "I'm only going because the Success brothers have some pretty good moves. I know they are going to put on a show. It's going to be a blowout.

-Kid 2: "Yea, you're right."

All the other kids agreed.

The time came for the game to start. It looks as if every kid in the neighborhood has come out to watch. It's two things that every person had in mind:

Fear and Failure were going to win.

The Success brothers were going to put on a good show while they lost.

The first game, Fear and Failure came out shooting like always. The Success brothers were no match for them. They lost by 40 points. Yes, that's right 40 big ones.

After the lost both, Believe and Conquer looked at one another.

-Believe: "Are you tired yet?"

-Conquer: "No."

They looked at Fear and Failure.

-Believe & Conquer: "Hey Fear and Failure… rematch?"

They started laughing, but they gave them what they asked for. Once again, they were beaten by 50 points. Repeatedly they would ask for a rematch, and repeatedly, they were beaten. That didn't stop them from playing again. After receiving many losses, the Believe brothers came up with a plan.

-Conquer: "We're going to ask for another rematch, but let's switch things up a little."

-Believe: I've watched how your opponent has guarded you, and I know that I can take him."

They both agreed that they would switch players this game. The rematch was set and another game was about to begin. This game was different. It was a lot different than all the other ones.

Fear and Failure would shoot.

The Success brothers would shoot.

Anything Fear and Failure did, the Success brothers duplicated *all the way down* to the end. The game was close. The neighborhood kids were on the edge of their seats.

Could it be that the Believe and Conquer could pull off something that had never been done before?

The Success brothers had the ball, and the score was 99 to 98 with Fear and Failure up by one point. This next shot for either side could make a difference. The Success brothers had the ball, and wanted to talk it over before the next play.

-Believe: "Listen, Fear is tired. This is what we're going to do. You inbound the ball, and I will give it back to you. I'm going to then run a little bit so Fear can't stay with me. You will give it back, and I will shoot the game-winning shot!"

The brothers agreed. It's now time to execute the plan. The ball was inbounded and passed back just like they planned. He started to run around just as he said. As Fear started to fall behind, he gets the ball back, and he launches the ball in the air. The crowd is looking on as the ball is floating in the air and into the bucket.

The crowd went crazy.

The neighborhood kids stormed the court excited that Fear and Failure had finally been beaten.

Just as the excitement starts to die down; a group of kids walked over to the Success brothers.

-Kid 1: "Hey Believe and Conquer brothers, great job beating Fear and Failure, but I have one question. What was going through your minds when you guys kept losing?"

The brothers looked at each other.

-Conquer: When we were playing, many times either my brother or I would ask each other, *are you tired yet*?

-Believe: If I can be honest, I was tired, wanted to quit, and even afraid. If you didn't know, Fear and Failure stood at about 6'3-6'5 while my brother and I only stand at about 5'8-5'10. No matter how I felt, when my brother asked me, *are you tired yet,* I had to get ready to play again. No matter what, I do not do anything without my brother. If my brother was ready to go again, I had to prepare my mind to play again. I was scared, tired, and wanted to quit.

-Conquer: The one thing that our parents taught us was to do everything together. See, my name is Conquer, and my brother name is Believe. I knew no matter how many times we lost, **if we could just believe, we could conquer**. What helped us to win was when we decided to change the game plan but never the mission.

In life, when you continue to get the same results, you do not quit. You figure out what worked and did not work. You use what works to win the mission. Never fear! When you fear, it is what leads to failure."

"Grandpa, I get it. I must always believe that no matter how many times I fail in life, if I just keep trying, I could conquer."

"That is right, Brandon. You must always remember it is not over until you quit. Believe and Conquer did not stop until they won."

The question I want to leave you with is this: ***Who runs your neighborhood?***

Your neighborhood is your MIND.

Who you allow to run it, is up to you. Either *fear and failure* or *believe and conquer*. You must always know who is in charge.

It is my deepest hope that you do not allow fear, which leads to failure, to take over your neighborhood (mind). I hope you believe through it all.

You will conquer.

Climbing Mount Success

Have you ever been told that you could not do something because it has never been done?

"What makes you think you could be the first?" They would ask.

You're not alone; I have been there.

I have realized in my many years of living, people would always put what they cannot do on you. The problem is that this comes from the people who we tend to love the most. People that we thought would have our backs. They tell us what we cannot or will never do.

Do you listen to them?

I found doing things out of your norm will always be the hardest. It is like building a house with no blueprint. You will find that others will always try to bring you down.

What is it that keeps you believing that you can conquer?

(Grandpa looked at Brandon.)

"I know that look from anywhere. What seems to be the problem?"

"Oh, it's nothing Grandpa."

"Well, the way you're looking is saying a lot, so go ahead, and tell me."

"Well, it's this kid in the neighborhood who is really fast, and no one has ever raced him and won. I told him I would be the first, and all the other kids laughed at me and called me a bunch of names. Maybe their right. What made me think I could be the first?!"

"You sound confident within yourself!"

(Grandpa walked over to Brandon.)

"Did I ever tell you about a good friend of mine who was the first to climb Mount Success? I think you will find you two are similar.

It was just before summer break, and all the students are sitting around the classroom. The teacher thought it would be a good idea to go around the class and ask every student what they had planned for the summer. She went around the room, pointing at the students one by one. Some said they were going to be with grandparents. Others said travel or getting a summer job. Everyone said what they were going to do except one student. This student was sitting in the corner by himself. He was known to be quiet. The teacher realized that she had asked everyone but him, what they had planned for the summer.

"I'm going to do something that has never been done before. I'm going to climb Mount Success."

The whole class laughed at him and called him a whole bunch of names.

"You're stupid, and you'll never make it to the top!"

No one had ever climbed Mount Success and made it to the top. He's now looking around the classroom at everyone laughing at him and thought to himself: *I will show them!*

Summer has now arrived, and they are out of school. He goes to the store, and he gets some hiking boots, knee pads, and a hiking stick. He got everything he needed, because he knew once he started, there was no turning back.

He is now beginning to climb the hill. Everything is going well when suddenly, he begins to realize the more he keeps climbing, the steeper the hill becomes. It is starting to feel like every step becomes harder and harder. The steeper he goes, the harder each step becomes.

His body is hurting, his legs are weak, and he doesn't know how far he has to go.

He keeps climbing.

Higher and higher he goes. His body is in pain. His legs are aching, but he continues to climb. As he's climbing, he sees this little area where he can take a small break. It is enough where he can sit down. As he's sitting, he looks up and sees that he still has a lot more climbing to do. As he is sitting, he starts to think to himself.

This is too much! I should just go back. They are right. It's a dumb idea. I will never make it to the top.

As he continues to sit, he then starts to think of how the class started laughing at him. He told them that he would be the first to not only climb Mount Success, but make it to the top. His attitude then changed, and he told himself: *You know what? I'm not going to rest to quit, but I'm going to rest to keep going because I still have more climbing to do.*

At this time, he remembered why he started in the first place. The next day after he rested, he started climbing again. The mountain is getting steeper and steeper.

His body begins hurting again.

His legs are aching, but he's still climbing.

He continues to keep climbing.

His body is hurting, but he's climbing.

He starts to get frustrated, but he keeps climbing. Step by step and pull by pull, he climbs. He is tired but still climbing. He doesn't know how much more he can take, but he never stops climbing.

He finally made it to the top. He's so worn out from climbing that he pulls himself up on the top of the mountain. He lays on his back with his eyes closed, because he is so beat up.

Aching and tired, he could barely feel his legs.

Trying to catch his breath, he opens his eyes.

He was so amazed at what he saw on the top of the mountain. He had never seen a scenery as amazing as what he saw. He heard birds chirping. He could see waterfalls into the river and the sun setting.

This place was so amazing he wanted to show everyone what he had seen. He started taking pictures of everything he had seen, especially pictures of himself being on the top of the mountain.

School is getting ready to start again. He made it down just in time to be in class on the first day. The teacher is happy to see the students, and she asked them, "What did you all do over the summer?"

This quiet little boy who sat in the corner, was now in the front of the class raising his hands to go first.

-Student: "I did something that has never been done before. **I climbed Mount Success.** Not only can I tell you but, I can show you."

He goes to the teacher's desk with the folder in hand. He lays out pictures of everything he saw while he was on top of this mountain. The class runs up to see the pictures.

They were so amazed at what they saw. They didn't know at the top of this mountain the scenery was so delightful. It was beautiful and pleasing to the eyes.

At the top of Mount Success, he was able to tell everyone that in order to see something like this, you have to climb to the top."

"Grandpa, I did not know you had a friend that was the first to ever climb Mount Success. That is a big mountain!"

"Yes, it is. Remember this, it does not matter what people say, it only matters what you tell yourself. If you believe you can beat him, you can."

(Brandon becomes assured.)

"You're right!"

"Wait! Where are you off to?!"

"I have a race to win!"

"Go get 'em!"

It was because Brandon believed he could that led him to not only challenge the fastest kid in the neighborhood; **HE WON** and became the first to ever do it.

If I can leave you with some very simple advice, it would be this:

On your way up, it will be hard, and it might seem ugly.

If you keep climbing to the top, there is a scenery that only you can capture if you choose to keep climbing."

The Gift of a Fruit Seed

(Brandon thinks to himself.)

Ugh. Why does Grandpa pick the hottest days to start planting some dumb seeds? I do not want to do this! All this digging, watering makes no sense.

"Grandpa, how come we just cannot go to the store and get what these seeds are?!"

"Son, it is not that easy. As a matter of fact, these seeds are not just seeds, these are special seeds, given to me as a gift, by a very special person and I promised them that I would take good care of them. Let me explain something to you. When someone gives you something, it is not to just be thrown to the side, but it is to be used. You were given something because you could use it in some type of way. It is what you do with it that makes it special. *(Grandpa laughs.)* I see you have a lot to learn. Sit down, let me tell you a story.

There were two farmers headed into town to get some seeds, because it was planting season. On the way, there they saw this huge sign that read "Free Fruit Seeds." They thought they would pull in and get some free seeds instead. As they were waiting in line, it was finally their time to get their seeds.

-Farmer 1: "What kind of seeds do you have?"

-Owner: "Well, I have all kinds. I have mango, oranges, apples, kiwi, and strawberries. I have just about any fruit you're looking for."

-Farmer 1: "I always wanted to plant apples. Let me get the apple seeds."

He takes the apple seeds and moves to the side so his friend could get a turn.

-Farmer 2: "What kind of seeds do you?"

-Owner: "Well, I have just about any seed you're looking for. I have mango, oranges, apples, kiwi, and strawberries. What would you like?"

-Farmer 2: "I always wanted to plant oranges. I will take the oranges seeds.

-Owner: "Here you go. Now boys, let me tell you something before you go plant the seeds that you have. These aren't just any seeds. These are special seeds. If I don't tell you anything else, whatever you do, take good care of these seeds."

They both received the seeds and headed back to the field where the seeds would be planted.

-Farmer 1: "You plant your seeds in this field, and I will plant mine in this field. This is so our seeds don't get tied in together."

They both agreed and went to plant their seeds. As they finished up, they met in the middle of the field.

-Farmer 1: "I am a little curious what made you pick orange seeds?"

-Farmer 2: "Oh man! I love orange juice, but not just any orange juice. I love fresh-squeezed orange juice. I thought if I planted them, I could have all the juice I want. What about you? Why did you pick apple seeds?"

-Farmer 1: "I love apple pie! I thought if I planted a field of apples, I could make all the apple pie I wanted, sit on my porch, and have me a nice slice every day if I liked."

There were a few steps they had to do to make it happen.

-Farmer 2: "This is what we must do to get the best out of our seed. Every day we must water, remove the weeds, and talk to our seed every day. If we do this, we will be having freshly squeezed orange juice and apple pie."

For a while, both of them, every day were watering, removing weeds, and talking to their seed just like they said.

One day, the one who planted the apples noticed that his friend *didn't* show up to tend to his seed. Day by day, he stopped showing up. He thought he would be a good friend and call him.

-Farmer 1: "Hey man! How is it going? I'm just calling because I noticed that you haven't come out to tend to your seed."

-Farmer 2: "Oh, yes, about that. I been so busy with everything else. I will be there tomorrow."

The next day, the one with apples shows up, and he does his normal routine. He waters, removes weeds, and talks to his seed.

His friend did not show up until later. He began walking to his field where he planted his oranges. To get to his field he had to first pass by the apple field.

He saw how his friend's field looked so nice. He knew for sure his field would look the same. He arrives at his field and realized that *nothing* has even grown from the ground.

While he was there, he watered, removed weeds, and talked to his seed. This would go on for a while. The one with apples would show up every day. The one with oranges would show up now and then.

It has finally come time for picking. They have both been watering, removing weeds, and talking to their seeds for some time now. Just like any day, the one with apples would arrive first.

When he got to his field, he was so amazed with his apples. They were a shining, bright red and ready to be eaten. He brought two big baskets with him ready to load as many apples as he could into them. When suddenly, his friend shows up with baskets as well. Along the way, he stops to see his friend loading apples into his baskets.

-Farmer 2: "Wow!!!! Your field has so many apples in it. I can't wait to get to my field and see all the great big oranges."

He rushes to his field, and to his surprise, nothing is there. He becomes upset and rushed back to the apple field where his friend is still loading apples in his basket.

-Farmer 2: "Hey!! How is it that you have so many apples, and I don't have a single orange?!"

Together they walked over to the orange field to see nothing as he said.

-Farmer 2: "I don't understand!! We planted these seeds at the same time, and yet I have nothing. You have more than you can bear?"

-Farmer 1: "Did your water your seed?"

-Farmer 2: "Every now and then. I was so busy I did not show up every day.

-Farmer 1: "Did you remove the bad weeds from around your seed?"

-Farmer 2: "I did not think that was necessary to do every time."

-Farmer 1: "Did you talk to your seed?"

-Farmer 2: "I did, but that's crazy. What do I look like talking to a seed?"

-Farmer 1: "Well, you asked me how I have so many apples, and you have nothing. The reason is because in order to get anything to grow, you must water it. *Water* is like practice. It helps it to grow and remain healthy. You have to remove the bad weeds. If you don't do this, it could **choke** the seed. It's like hanging around people that are not going to help you grow. You must **constantly** remove bad people from your life. **You have to talk to your seed.** You have to tell it what it is before it even **becomes** that. You must tell your seed just how bright the future looks. I am to fill my baskets full of my apples, because I *constantly* watered… *constantly* removed the bad weeds from around my seed… and *I told my seed it was an apple at the time it was only a seed."*

"So Grandpa, that is why these seeds were so important to you, because they knew you would take good care of the seeds?"

"That is right! I want to plant these seeds because I want to show them what they gave me did not go to waste. How you show that is by giving them back what the seed produces."

When you have a gift, *you must take very good care of it.* You must water it, and this will make it grow.

The time you put in to make it better, you will always have to remove negative people out our life. These are people who will not help you grow and will only stop you from your growth. Be very careful because these people seem to be very close to you.

Talk to your seed.

This is important because you must tell yourself what you are before you become whatever it is. It is not what people say that matters, but what you tell yourself *only matters*.

After taking the apples home, he did exactly what he said. He made an apple pie. The pie and it ended up being so good. He had so many apples left over, that he made pies for others to try. His pie ended up being some of the best apple pie in the whole city. People from all around started to hear and wanted to try for themselves. He started an apple pie business, and it all started with a seed that was given to him.

I want you to remember this. We are all given a special seed at birth. It is your job to water it, remove the bad weeds from around it, and talk to it in order to help your seed (gift) grow.

***What you do it with is what makes the seed
special.***

In the Air, FINALLY!

How come we are not in the air yet?

Have you realized anytime you buy something that must be built that it comes with instructions?

Instructions are usually a step by step guide that helps you put everything together to be done the right way.

Can you think of a time that you rushed something?

How did it turn out?

If you are anything like me, *rushing always caused me to mess up.*

"Grandpa, I cannot get this dumb plane to get off the ground."

"Did you read the instructions?"

"I do not have to do all that."

"Son, you have to read! You cannot just take the toy plane out the box, and expect it to just go in the air. It doesn't work like that."

"But Grandpa."

"But nothing! If you think that's what it takes, then you are sadly mistaking. Come here! Let me teach you something.

It was the first time I had ever ridden on a plane. I was so excited I couldn't think straight. I was going to Miami, Florida to layout on the beach. I wanted to have a nice, cool drink and get some sun. I was so excited. I told everyone that it would be my first time on the plane and that I was headed to Miami. The day finally arrived. I was getting ready to leave for Miami. My flight was at 2:30 pm I was so excited I arrived at the airport at 12pm. I arrived early so that I would make it on time to leave at 2:30. Now, I'm waiting to board the plane at the gate. Sitting next to me, are other people who look as if they were headed to Florida themselves. I expressed to them how it was my first time ever being on a plane and in Miami. I told them how I couldn't wait to check into my hotel and layout on the beach with a nice, cool drink. Can you tell I was ready?

We were finally getting ready to board the plane. I'm now all in line telling everyone how excited I was to get on the plane and can't wait until it takes off. More importantly, I couldn't wait to get to the beach and enjoy myself.

I finally found my seat. I laid back a little and got comfortable. Just before we took off, the pilot comes over the intercom system.

-Hostess: "Good evening, ladies and gentlemen! We are discovering a few errors in our system, but we will take off shortly when the problem is fixed. Thank you!"

The time is now 3:00 pm. I am looking at my watch wondering what is taking so long.

Now it's 4:00 pm.

I look again, and it's 4:30 pm

I started to become impatient. I jumped up and the flight attendant quickly comes to sit me down. At this moment, I'm frustrated and ready to take off.

-Grandpa: "What's going on with the plane? We were supposed to be in the air a long time ago. I am supposed to be on the beach enjoying myself, and yet I'm still here."

-Flight Attendant: "Sir, will you please calm down and sit down in your seat?"

I sat down for a second, but we still haven't gotten in the air yet. Another hour goes by, and I start to get even more upset.

-Grandpa: "I want this plane in the air right now! It's taking too long. I'm supposed to be on the beach right now."

The pilot hears all the fussing in the back and knew it was best if he checked it out.

-Pilot: "What seems to be the problem?"

-Grandpa: "This plane was supposed to be in the air a long time ago, but we're still here on the ground."

-Pilot: "Yes sir, I understand that, but I did come on the intercom to say that we had a small delay with the system."

-Grandpa: "That was hours ago."

-Pilot: "Yes, I understand, but I did say until the problem was fixed, we wouldn't be in the air."

-Grandpa: "I don't care right now! I'm supposed to be on the beach enjoying myself."

-Pilot: "Yes, I get that too, but the problem is that you're so focused on the take off of the plane that you don't see what it takes to get a plane off the ground. In order for me to get this plane off the ground, I have to make sure I know how many people are on the plane. I have to make sure all the luggage is on the plane. I have to make sure I have enough fuel to get me to our destination. I also have to make sure that my signal reaches the cell tower for communication. I would hate for a minor problem on the ground to become a major problem in the air."

After the pilot spoke, I started to realize that I didn't think about what it took to even get the plane off the ground. I was so focused on getting to my destination because *I was excited.*

-Grandpa: "You're right. I was so focused on getting to my destination that I didn't think about the steps that it takes to get the plane off the ground."

-Pilot: "It's okay to be excited. Everything takes time and the right steps in order to make it work." Remember this, focus on what it takes to get whatever it is you want done. For me no matter how long it takes I want to make sure that I had everything ready for take off."

-Flight Attendant: Alright ladies and gentlemen. We are all set for take-off. If you will, please take your seats. We're going to ride this baby like we stole it.

The pilot hears the good news and rushes to the front. I sat down in my seat to prepare for take-off.

You see, Brandon, that is why it is important for you to take steps to where you are trying to go. Could you image if the pilot would have just taken off, it could have cost a lot of harm to the people on broad."

"You're right! That could have been some serious damage. Oh, look, Grandpa! I found a missing piece."

Brandon places it in the toy plane, and it takes off in the air.

Often in life, we focus so much on getting to a place when we should be focused on what it takes to get to where we hope to be.

Can you imagine if the pilot knew he wasn't receiving a signal with the cellular tower and still took off anyway?

The pilot knew for his safety and the passengers on the plane that no matter how long it took, he wanted to make sure that the plane was ready for take-off.

I want you to understand that this is saying to not take risks. You must make sure that you take *steps* when you're taking risks. You must know what you're up against before you do whatever it is your heart desires.

What It Takes to be Successful

"Whatever you do, just see it through."

It simply means whatever you start. I dare you to finish.

Think Success
Take Action
Be Committed
See It
Focus
Sacrifice
Get Up

What It Takes to be Successful List

On the previous page, I gave you the 1st 7 Steps to give you a start. Seven completes a cycle, but let's go deeper.

1. Stop dreaming and start *taking action*.
2. *Be committed* to the process.
3. Do not worry about what others do not see. It only matters *what you see*.
4. *Stay focused.*
5. You will always have to *sacrifice.*
6. No matter how many times you are knocked down, *keep getting up.*
7. *Success starts* in your mind.
8. Do not rest to quit, but *rest to keep going*.
9. You must *water*, remove weeds, and *talk* to your gift.
   a. Water - to make it grow.
   b. Remove - always remove people that will not help you grow.
   c. Talk and tell yourself what you are before you become that.
10. Do not rush it, but take the necessary steps. Remember, nothing happens overnight.

Meet the Author

Brandon Oliver Sr. is the founder and chief executive officer of John Eunice Inspiration. He is a motivational speaker who narrates original stories that would make you think, act, or do a thing. He helps individuals by encouraging them, motivating them, inspiring them as well as uplifting them. With a reach from the young to the aged and the world at large, he wholeheartedly speaks to them about the power of never giving up. Brandon believes that motivating and inspiring individuals will help them change their mindset about success. He takes them through a motivational journey where they will begin to appreciate every encounter in their life and work towards accomplishing their goals regardless of what they face.

Brandon is a trained leader with the completion of academic studies at Kansas Christian College. Being a Chief Executive Officer and inspirational speaker is a great honor, and he views that as one of the most significant awards he will ever receive.

Connect with the Author

Visit the website: www.johneunice.com

Facebook: **Brandon Oliver**

Instagram: **Brandonspeaks5**

Email: Binspired52@gmail.com

YouTube: **When Brandon Speaks**

The Author's "Inspiration Corner"
(All quotes are by the Author, Brandon Oliver)

"

You are what you tell yourself.
I am strong. I will succeed.
I will not give up, I will keep going.
If you say it, believe it!
IT WILL BE!
KEEP MOVING FORWARD!!!

"

"

The beginning of success
is always the hardest, but you
MUST KEEP GOING!!!

"

"

Whatever you do, just see it through. It simply means whatever you start, I dare you to finish.

"

"

Wake Up. Get Dress.
LET'S GO TO WORK!!!
#DressForSuccess

"

"

Stay positive, motivated and keep being great.

"

Take Notes of Your Favorite Stories

Take Notes of Your Favorite Stories

Handwritten Sentiments from the Author

www.ingramcontent.com/pod-product-compliance
Lightning Source LLC
Chambersburg PA
CBHW070516090426
42735CB00012B/2799